CLASS 70 LOCOMOTIVES

John Jackson

AMBERLEY

First published 2017

Amberley Publishing
The Hill, Stroud
Gloucestershire, GL5 4EP

www.amberley-books.com

Copyright © John Jackson, 2017

The right of John Jackson to be identified as
the Author of this work has been asserted in
accordance with the Copyrights, Designs and
Patents Act 1988.

ISBN 978 1 4456 7272 4 (print)
ISBN 978 1 4456 7273 1 (ebook)

British Library Cataloguing in Publication Data.
A catalogue record for this book is available from
the British Library.

Origination by Amberley Publishing.
Printed in the UK.

Introduction

This book gives a photographic account of the thirty-six locomotives in use today (June 2017), together with a look back at some of their workings over the last few years. But first, a brief resume of the Class 70 fleet history over its first ten years of UK operations.

It was towards the end of 2007 that Freightliner announced its 'Project Genesis' – a new beginning for the company. It was an attempt by the company to procure locomotives that could offer improved fuel efficiency without reducing the loco's haulage abilities. These locos were to run alongside Freightliner's older stablemates.

General Electric was announced as the preferred manufacturer and in the summer of 2009 construction work started on a batch of twenty six-axle Co-Co PowerHaul locos at its base in Erie, Pennsylvania, USA. (There was also an option for Freightliner to acquire a further ten machines, which was not subsequently taken up.)

This Class was to be allocated the designation 'Class 70' within the Total Operating Processing System ('TOPS'). In the days of British Rail, this class number had been used for a small class of electric locos but there is absolutely no other connection. Historically, the 70s number range had generally been allocated to electric locos. This Class 70 TOPS coding for a diesel engine type therefore bucked this trend.

The Class 70 locomotives have a 3,690 hp engine and a maximum speed of 120 km/h (75 mph).

Towards the end of 2009, the first two locos (No. 70001 and No. 70002) were unloaded at Newport Docks and shortly afterwards the former loco received the name *PowerHaul*. I recall that my first impression on seeing these locos was, 'similar to the earlier Class 58s in design and appearance'.

Freightliner was soon to test No. 70001 on a thirty-wagon intermodal to and from Felixstowe. They claimed this test a success shortly afterwards. Not to be outdone, loco No. 70002 was tested on a 1,300-ton coal working consisting of nineteen loaded hoppers at around the same time. It was to be used in revenue-earning service at the beginning of December 2009 on coal traffic between Stoke Gifford and Rugeley Power Station.

This two-loco consignment was followed by further deliveries, which included loco No. 70012. On 5 January 2011, this engine suffered the now infamous fate of falling during the unloading process from the *Beluga Endurance* at Newport Docks and incurring considerable damage. It therefore never turned a wheel in revenue-earning service in the UK. It was instead returned, unused by Freightliner, to General Electric. Its twisted frame was straightened by GE and it has subsequently been used as a test bed.

Other locos have made the headlines since then. In 2012, both No. 70014 and No. 70018 were the victims of fire damage. In April that same year, No. 70018 suffered an engine room fire in the Micheldever area in Hampshire. No. 70014 was out of traffic for over a year after suffering an electrical fire in autumn 2012.

In October 2012, loco No. 70099 arrived at Newport Docks. This was a 'demonstrator' locomotive, which, numbered as DE 37001 under the Turkish numbering system, was a joint venture between General Electric and Turkish company Tulomsas. Its transition to a UK loco took a number of months. The necessary modifications carried out for it to run in the UK were handled by Loughborough-based company Brush (now a subsidiary of Wabtec).

In late 2013, Colas Rail announced it would be taking up Freightliner's order option of ten locomotives. These were to be allocated numbers from 70801 upwards. This demonstrator (No. 70099) was renumbered within this number range and became No. 70801. It, therefore, formed the first loco of this order. It had arrived in the UK carrying a dark green livery and the repaint into Colas colours was completed in 2014 by Cardiff's Canton paint shops. The remaining nine locomotives were to be delivered from Erie, Pennsylvania, during the first half of 2014. These were to carry the numbers 70802 to 70810 inclusive.

No. 70802 was to break new ground for its class in July 2014. Colas Rail has a contract to move timber from Carlisle to Kronospan's plant at Chirk in North Wales and this was to be the first occasion that one of these trains would be hauled by a Class 70 (paired with a Class 66). The 70 was to be removed at Warrington on this inaugural run.

A further seven Class 70 locomotives were ordered by Colas in 2015. These were to be numbered from 70811 to 70817 inclusive.

Also in 2015, Freightliner Group Ltd was acquired by US-based Genesis & Wyoming Inc.

During 2016, two Colas locos suffered collision/accident damage. In February, No. 70803 was derailed, along with two wagons, following a collision near Ivybridge in Devon. It managed to reach Plymouth under its own power before spending many months out of traffic awaiting parts. No. 70804 was also to be derailed after 'running away'; this time the location was Toton, in November.

The 2015 order was fulfilled in the spring of 2017. First, No. 70812 arrived at the end of February, surprisingly on its own. It was then followed shortly afterwards by the delivery of No. 70811 and No. 70813. The order was completed by the arrival of *Atlantic Cartier* at Seaforth Docks on 18 April 2017, conveying Nos 70814 to 70817. These four locos were moved to Crewe on 3 May 2017.

So, at the beginning of May 2017, the UK fleet stood at a total of thirty-six locomotives – nineteen operated by Freightliner (numbered 70001–70011 and 70013–70020) and seventeen operated by Colas (numbered 70801–70817). That said, the dramatic downturn in coal traffic operated by Freightliner resulted in several of their examples stored out of use at their Leeds' Midland Road depot. A 'snapshot' of the fleet position on a Monday morning in May shows:

Nos 70001, 70002, 70009, 70013, 70016 and 70018 stored at Midland Road.
Nos 70006, 70007, 70008 and 70010 undergoing exams/maintenance at the same depot.
No. 70014 on exam at Ipswich.
The remaining eight examples allocated to various freightliner container workings (and none on 'heavyhaul' work). The container traffic included Freightliner's recently acquired Russell Logistics traffic between Daventry and Coatbridge. No. 70011 was showing on that day's southbound working (although it is predominantly pairs of Class 90s that work on these services).

A similar glance at the Colas Rail pool of seventeen locos on that same typical Monday morning shows:

Eight examples stabled at Cardiff Canton, four stabled at Westbury (Wiltshire) and one each at Aberthaw (South Wales), Grangemouth (Central Scotland) and Barnetby (South Humberside). Several of these were showing as for examination or maintenance.
Just two examples were on the move at this time and both were on infrastructure trains. One was from Westbury to Bescot (West Midlands) and the other was from Hoo Junction

(in Kent) to Whitemoor (Cambs). There were two other Colas class members at work the previous day (Sunday) on engineering traffic in the Bristol area.

At the time of writing, the Colas examples of the class were regular performers on the company's infrastructure duties in conjunction with Network Rail, but they were also spreading their wings on more general freight duties. Examples of this were:

Loco No. 70816 was briefly stabled at Barnetby and received a run on the tank traffic from Lindsey Oil Refinery on South Humberside to Rectory Junction (near Nottingham).

Loco No. 70802 was dispatched to Grangemouth in Scotland. Its use has included the cement movement from Oxwellmains (near Dunbar in East Lothian) to Aberdeen and the transport of aviation fuel tanks to Glasgow's Prestwick Airport.

For a few months now Colas Class 70 locos have been the power provided on a regular movement of powdered cement from Aberthaw Cement Plant to both Westbury and Moorswater (near Liskeard in Cornwall).

More recently, Colas has commenced a flow of dredged sand from Neath in South Wales, alternating to destinations at Washwood Heath (West Midlands) and Stourton, near Leeds. Again, Class 70 locos would appear to be their power of choice for these workings.

Only time will tell if the future is brighter for these Colas examples than for the earlier Freightliner ones, and whether this expansion of duties for the Colas locos will continue.

Meanwhile, the fate of the six Freightliner locos at Leeds Midland Road remains unknown. Will the remainder still be confined to container traffic? Much will depend on loco reliability. Since completion of deliveries, I doubt there has been a day when all nineteen locos were available for traffic.

A glance at the locations featured in this book will give the best guide as to where to see Class 70 locos. When not at work, the Freightliner examples are most likely to be found at Leeds Midland Road, Crewe Basford Hall or at the two principal container port stabling points – Southampton Maritime and Ipswich (for Felixstowe). Their day-to-day workings are almost entirely restricted to use on such container trains, mainly to and from these two ports.

The Colas Rail locos, when not working, tend to be found grouped where infrastructure demands are at their greatest. Particularly likely locations include Cardiff (Canton depot area), Westbury, Eastleigh (near Southampton), Hoo Junction, near Higham in Kent, and Bescot in the West Midlands.

A glance through the pages of this book will help identify 'hotspots' that offer the best chances of seeing both operators' locos at work through the same location, but the areas of overlap between the two companies are limited. By overlaying the routes taken by Colas Rail's regular weekday infrastructure trains with the map of regular Freightliner services, a few candidates emerge.

Locations such as Nuneaton, Eastleigh, the line between Didcot and Leamington Spa, and the London suburbs offer, perhaps, the best chance. With the class limited to thirty active members nationally, there are, of course, no guarantees.

Freightliner's first Class 70 loco was No. 70001 and it arrived in the UK in late 2009. It is seen here stabled at one of Freightliner's main bases, Leeds Midland Road, on 23 June 2015. Pictured in the company of No. 66617, the photo was taken from a unit passing the depot on a Wakefield Kirkgate to Leeds service.

Colas Rail's first Class 70 was No. 70801. It had previously been a demonstrator for Turkish-based Tulomsas under their number DE 37001. On arrival in the UK it was numbered 70099. Renumbering and repainting followed and it entered service for Colas in 2013. The loco is seen here passing through Nuneaton, working from Westbury to Bescot on 19 March 2014.

Container traffic to and from the ports of Southampton and Felixstowe is the mainstay work for the Freightliner examples of the class. Here No. 70007 heads north through Nuneaton on 2 June 2015 with a Southampton to Trafford Park working.

No. 70004 was seen heading in the opposite direction on 7 September 2015. This southbound working was from Crewe to Felixstowe via the West Coast Main Line (WCML). It is seen here approaching Bletchley station.

Another southbound freightliner is seen here behind No. 70018 through Nuneaton on 2 September 2015. This time the working is from Ditton (on Merseyside) to Felixstowe. This working will take the West Coast Main Line (WCML) to North London before heading eastwards along the Great Eastern Main Line (GEML).

Some workings from the Suffolk port of Felixstowe take the route across East Anglia to Peterborough rather than via the London suburbs. No. 70020 is seen here approaching Nuneaton from the Leicester line on 19 January 2016 with a Felixstowe to Crewe liner.

By contrast to Freightliner's workings, Colas Rail's Class 70s are chiefly to be found on engineer's workings in connection with Network Rail's infrastructure work. On 20 May 2014, No. 70807 passes Water Orton, on the outskirts of Birmingham, with a Westbury to Bescot that will take the Sutton Park freight-only line to reach its destination.

The Monday to Thursday Westbury to Bescot often has no northbound wagons to move. One such occasion was on 9 May 2015. No. 70809 is therefore working light engine when seen at Leamington Spa. It should return with a rake of wagons later in the day.

By contrast, a Monday is often a good bet for the movement of point carriers from either Westbury or Hinksey (near Oxford). After weekend engineering work they are tripped back to the yard at Beeston, near Nottingham, via Bescot and Toton. On 29 February 2016, a Monday, No. 70808 heads such a rake through Nuneaton.

It's No. 70804's turn to be captured on this working on 14 September 2015. It is seen passing through Oxford with a mixed assortment of wagons that day.

No. 70003 spent some time out of traffic at Leeds Midland Road depot in 2016/2017. By 26 June 2017 it had returned to main-line duties. On that date it passed through Nuneaton on a northbound freightliner from Felixstowe to Crewe.

This double-headed working pausing for a crew change offers a comparison of cab sides with the Class 70's stablemate, Class 66. Nos 70007 and 66504, in revised livery, are the liner haulage through Nuneaton on 6 September 2016.

Two freightliner Class 70 locos were to carry names. First to be named was No. 70001. It is seen on 2 May 2014 carrying the name *Powerhaul*.

The second naming was on loco No. 70004 in February 2011. It is seen here on 8 June 2016 carrying the name *The Coal Industry Society*. Ironically, it was the sudden and dramatic downturn in coal traffic that was surely a contributory factor in six of the Freightliner sub-class being stored in 2017.

One of Freightliner's main stabling points is adjacent to Ipswich station. This is, of course, convenient for its activity at the nearby Felixstowe Docks. On 2 May 2014, No. 70001 is to be found stabled there between its liner duties.

With at least three of its Class 66 stablemates for company, No. 70009 is found stabled adjacent to Ipswich station, alongside No. 66565, on 28 November 2012.

On 8 July 2015 it's the turn of both No. 70007 and No. 70019 to be found at this Suffolk stabling point.

With a solitary Class 66 'over the back', No. 70011 is seen on the Ipswich stabling point on 29 September 2016, awaiting its next Felixstowe-related duty.

Colas Rail has an important south of England base at Hoo Junction, just north of Higham in Kent. Regular weekday Colas-operated infrastructure trains run from the yard here to and from Whitemoor (Cambridgeshire) and Eastleigh (near Southampton). While its small pool of five Class 66 locos often work these trains, it is just as likely they will produce Class 70 haulage. On 11 November 2015, haulage for the Whitemoor train was entrusted to No. 70802. Its rake of ageing 'seacows' offer a marked contrast to the 'new' locomotive. They are seen heading for Whitemoor through Bowes Park on the Hertford loop.

On 29 June 2015 it's the turn of No. 70801 to provide the haulage. Its mixed rake is seen approaching Gospel Oak, again on the Whitemoor-bound service.

Also on 29 June 2015, the Eastleigh working was entrusted to No. 70803. Its route takes it snake-like around London, including through Clapham Junction (here), as it heads towards Eastleigh.

The Eastleigh-bound working is seen at Clapham Junction again on 30 April 2015. No. 70810 is just about to pass through the Reading line platforms with a rake of side tippers.

As already mentioned, liner services between Crewe and Felixstowe run either via the WCML and around North London, or cross-country via Leicester and Peterborough. On 3 March 2016, No. 70015 takes the former route and is seen heading south through Bletchley.

On 15 May 2017, No. 70011 takes the same routing and is also seen heading through Bletchley, bound for Felixstowe Docks.

Freightliner's No. 70015 was viewed at Marholm (just north of Peterborough) on 9 July 2016. It is heading a Felixstowe Docks to Crewe liner. The train will shortly leave the ECML and head west towards Leicester to join the WCML at Nuneaton.

Then, two months later, 26 September 2016 saw No. 70011 approach Leicester as it heads south and then west on another Felixstowe to Crewe working.

Westbury (in Wiltshire) is one of Colas Rail's engineering train hubs with Class 70 locos regularly stabled in the yard there. On 15 July 2014, No. 70801 is awaiting its next duty.

On 25 May 2014, a visit over the Spring Bank Holiday weekend proved to be more productive. No. 70806 arrived on a returning engineer's train at Sunday lunchtime.

Shortly afterwards, No. 70808 arrived with another returning infrastructure train. No. 70805 and No. 70807 were also to be found there and remained unused that day.

Freightliner Class 70s share the haulage burden on their Anglo-Scottish service linking Daventry (Northamptonshire) with Coatbridge (east of Glasgow). Class 66s and pairs of Class 90s also make appearances. On 16 March 2016, No. 70006 is pictured at Rugby on the final stretch of its southbound journey into Daventry.

On 27 January 2017, the northbound working is seen passing through Nuneaton in the hands of No. 70004.

The same loco was in charge again a month or so later on 27 February 2017. This time the northbound working is seen coming through Tamworth's low level platforms.

On 8 May 2017, the northbound working was in the hands of No. 70007. On this occasion it passed through Nuneaton on the down fast line.

The Colas infrastructure working from Westbury to Bescot often sees more than one Class 70 in the consist. For example, on 21 October 2014, No. 70802 leads No. 70810 through Nuneaton.

On 18 June 2015, it's the turn of No. 70809 and No. 70805 as the double-headed combination passed through Nuneaton with a rake of mainly JNA wagons.

No. 70805 appeared again on 12 January 2016. This time its classmate, No. 70806, was leading as it passed through Nuneaton.

Three locos made an appearance on 7 July 2016. No. 70801 leads No. 70807 and No. 70809 as the working passes through Nuneaton.

Light engine moves remain inevitable on today's railway. No. 70005 is seen waiting for the road north from Sheffield on 21 May 2014. It is running from Earles Sidings in Derbyshire's Hope Valley to the Freightliner depot at Leeds Midland Road.

On 15 April 2016, No. 70003 heads south through Nuneaton on a move from Freightliner's Basford Hall base at Crewe to the container terminal at Daventry in Northamptonshire.

A month or so earlier, on 14 March 2016, No. 70011 heads light engine in the opposite direction, working from Daventry back to Freightliner's Basford Hall stabling point in Crewe.

A much longer light engine move involved No. 70002 on 13 October 2013. It is seen working from Aldwarke (near Rotherham in South Yorkshire) back to its Crewe Basford Hall base. It will take a circuitous route to its destination but it is seen here passing through Chesterfield station not long after commencing its journey.

Given the proximity of the container port at Southampton, Eastleigh sees its fair share of Class 70 activity. On 30 August 2013, No. 70013 waits in Eastleigh station for the signal north on a freightliner service to Trafford Park in Manchester.

A year later, on 14 July 2014, No. 70020 is approaching the same signal. This time the destination is Merseyside for this container train from Southampton to Garston, routed initially via Basingstoke and Reading.

In the early afternoon of 29 April 2017, two Class 70 locos were seen heading towards Southampton within the space of a couple of hours. First, No. 70005 passes Eastleigh's East Yard with a working from Garston to Southampton. It is followed almost exactly two hours later by No. 70011. This time the Southampton-bound service had commenced its journey from Crewe's Basford Hall yard.

The date is again 30 August 2013 in this view from Eastleigh. No. 70017 is to be found out of action within the Works area with Freightliner wagons and South Eastern electric unit stock for company.

Colas Rail are also regular operators in the Eastleigh area. This makes it an ideal place to view the movements of Class 70 locos from the two different companies. On the morning of 3 October 2015, No. 70803 is to be found stabled in the loco holding sidings adjacent to the station platform. On this occasion, its companions are a GBRf Class 66/7 and a Class 73.

Later that day it was to be joined in Eastleigh East Yard by stablemate No. 70807. This loco had arrived light engine from Westbury and was also to be used on weekend engineering duties in the area.

On the following morning, 4 October 2013, No. 70803 itself was to be seen heading out of Eastleigh's East Yard on a rake of new concrete sleepers. It was to take the curve south-east of the station towards Botley on its way to a possession (a protected section of rail during engineering work).

The use of Freightliner Class 70s on infrastructure duties has become increasingly less common. Back on 15 May 2013, No. 70002 was seen heading south through Crewe station on a rake conveying redundant sleepers.

On 8 June 2016, No. 70004 was seen heading in the opposite direction through Stafford. This time its rake of IFAs contains new concrete sleepers. The working is from Cemex Rail Products' base at Washwood Heath (West Midlands) to Crewe.

The same loco, No. 70004, is again featured in this view from Water Orton on the outskirts of Birmingham. It was seen on 1 October 2013 with its rake of JNAs passing the platform end – with evidence of other photographers present! This working, from Crewe to Toton (via Bescot), is currently in the hands of Direct Rail Services (DRS).

Another working currently in the hands of DRS is the regular weekday ballast working involving empties from Crewe being tripped to Mountsorrel (Leicestershire) for loading and return. Back on 1 May 2013, this was another working that regularly featured Freightliner Class 70s. No. 70015 is seen passing through Loughborough shortly after leaving Mountsorrel with the loaded return working, which reached the WCML via Burton-on-Trent and the Lichfield Trent Valley curve.

The Colas Class 70-hauled Westbury to Bescot is renowned for the variety of wagons that are to be found in its consist. It also lays over in Hinksey yard (just south of Oxford) where its onward consist is often changed. On 18 January 2017 it reached Nuneaton with just three wagons in tow. It is seen about to be overhauled by a northbound Class 66-hauled Freightliner working.

On 25 January 2016, the consist was a very different one. On conversion to MXAs, these wagons also received a new coat of paint. Their red colouring makes a striking contrast with the loco's own livery even on a gloomy afternoon. No. 70810 heads the working through Nuneaton.

On 19 May 2014, No. 70807's consist was formed, unusually, of High Output Ballast Cleaner wagons. The lengthy train is seen passing through Nuneaton.

Yet another wagon variation can be seen in this shot of No. 70805 on 6 March 2014. It is seen passing through Nuneaton this time with a rake of 'salmons'. These bogie rail wagons date back to the 1950s and 1960s.

Freightliner Class 70s continue to be frequent performers in the London suburbs. They make regular appearances on the liners that use the southern end of the WCML and the North London line to reach Stratford in East London. The latter station is the location on 24 July 2014 as No. 70013 heads west towards the North London line on an unidentified working.

In this view, No. 70003 has already taken this route through the London suburbs. On 26 May 2017 it heads north through Harrow & Wealdstone on the WCML with a liner from Felixstowe to Lawley Street (Birmingham).

A couple of years earlier, on 24 September 2015, No. 70017 is seen in virtually the same spot as it heads north through Harrow & Wealdstone. This time its load from Felixstowe is bound for Crewe.

London freightliners often lay over at Brent Sidings, Willesden, before continuing their journeys. One such example is seen here on 26 May 2017. No. 70006 is pausing on a Trafford Park to Felixstowe working. It is glimpsed from a Milton Keynes Central to East Croydon service passing on an adjacent line.

Deliveries of new Colas Class 70s have reached the UK via Liverpool's Seaforth Docks. On 3 June 2014, newly delivered No. 70810 was running light engine from the docks to Bescot Yard in the West Midlands. It is seen here heading south through Stafford station.

Pontypool & New Inn rarely gets a mention among the enthusiast fraternity. It did, however, on 19 May 2016. That day, a working from there to Colas Rail's base in Rugby appeared on the list of scheduled workings through Nuneaton. After much speculation as to what it might be, No. 70801 appeared, dragging a Colas-operated track machine numbered DR73805 south onto the WCML towards its Rugby destination.

The sharp decline in coal traffic on the network has meant that Colas Class 70s have seen little work on such trains. In 2015, they did handle a flow from Portbury Docks (Bristol) to the power station at Ratcliffe (Nottinghamshire). On 13 March that year, No. 70809 heads the returning empties through Tamworth (High Level).

A couple of weeks later, on 26 March 2015, it's the turn of No. 70810 on this working. This rake of former Freightliner 'heavyhaul' wagons was outbased at Gloucester between workings. The Class 70 is heading for the yard there as it too is seen passing through Tamworth (High Level).

Freightliner has a choice of routes for its container traffic leaving Southampton in order to reach Garston on Merseyside. On 28 June 2017, No. 70015 hauled a northbound working through Stafford. It had reached here via Reading, West London and the WCML.

Three years earlier and regular Class 70 duties included handling the cement traffic to and from Earles Sidings in Derbyshire's Hope Valley. On 3 September 2014, No. 70011 accelerates north from Bedford station following a crew change there. On this occasion it was returning to Earles Sidings with a rake of empties from Theale (near Reading).

Class 70s were also regular visitors through Sheffield on these workings to and from Earles Sidings. On 15 November 2015, No. 70002 heads eastwards through the station working from Earles to Drax Power Station.

Freightliner Class 70s were regularly seen on light engine movements through Sheffield. After a period outbased at Earles, the locos were tripped to and from their main base at Leeds Midland Road. On 19 September 2013, No. 70003 is in convoy with No. 66618 on one such move back to their Leeds depot.

As already mentioned, there are two regular weekday infrastructure diagrams that Colas operate from their base at Hoo Junction in Kent. These operate to Eastleigh (near Southampton) and to Whitemoor (Cambridgeshire). On 4 November 2014, No. 70803 appears around the corner at Willesden Junction's high level platform, heading for Whitemoor.

On 3 April 2017, the same working is operated by No. 70804. This time it is seen passing along the side of Hornsey station and is about to take the Hertford loop on its way to Whitemoor.

The Eastleigh-bound working takes the Reading line platforms as it heads through Clapham Junction. On 7 May 2015, No. 70806 is in charge of the working, with long welded rail carriers among its consist.

On 3 April 2017 it's the turn of No. 70809 to provide the diesel traction. It is seen on the curve approaching Clapham Junction with a lengthy consist.

The downturn in coal traffic on our railways today means that the sight of a Freightliner Class 70 at the head of a rake of heavyhaul coal hoppers has all but disappeared. Back on 3 December 2012, No. 70016 is at the head of a return working taking empty hoppers from Ratcliffe Power Station back to Daw Mill Colliery. The Warwickshire colliery, the last in the West Midlands, was closed in 2013 following fire damage. The empties are seen here passing through nearby Nuneaton.

A month later, on 5 January 2015, No. 70005 heads another rake of empty coal hoppers on the same circuit. It was not realised at the time that these workings had but a few weeks left to run. This Ratcliffe to Daw Mill working is seen heading south through Leicester station.

On 7 July 2013, No. 70013 is stabled in Stoke Gifford yard, near Bristol, in the company of some of the familiar Freightliner coal hoppers. This yard is situated alongside Bristol Parkway station. Several rakes were staged here between workings from the nearby docks at Avonmouth and Portbury. Sister engine No. 70011 can be glimpsed alongside No. 70013.

May 2017 saw the delivery of Nos 70814, 70815, 70816 and 70817. They were again delivered to the UK via the docks at Seaforth, Liverpool. Shortly after delivery, they had reached Bescot Yard. By the time this photo was taken, No. 70816 had already left light engine, bound for Barnetby on South Humberside. That left this trio, stabled here on 5 May 2017. No. 70816 had reached Doncaster by that date, as evidenced elsewhere in this book.

No. 70815 was at the Tame Bridge (south) end of the convoy within Bescot's Engineer's Yard.

No. 70814 is seen at the centre of the trio of Class 70s, flanked by No. 70815 and No. 70817.

No. 70817 was at the Bescot (north) end of the convoy.

Freightliner's regular daily services include the important link between the deep sea port at Southampton and Manchester's terminal at Trafford Park. This journey of approximately 200 miles each way is undertaken several times a day using both Class 66 and Class 70 locomotives, with a crew change usually taking place at Nuneaton. On 3 June 2015, this northbound working is in the hands of No. 70007.

On 5 May 2016, the same northbound service is entrusted to No. 70014. It is again seen slowing for a crew change on the platform in Nuneaton station.

On 12 May 2015 it's the turn of No. 70009. Just to keep the enthusiasts – and photographers – as well as the staff on their toes, there was a last minute switch to platform 2 for the crew change that day!

This working is also used to move locos between Freightliner's various UK depots. On the occasion of 18 April 2017, No. 66571 is the leading locomotive. It is seen here giving No. 70010 a lift, probably to Freightliner's Basford Hall depot in Crewe.

In 2016, Colas Rail commenced a regular flow of cement traffic from Aberthaw in South Wales. Some days the working is to Westbury in Wiltshire. Once a week, however, it heads much further afield to Moorswater, near Liskeard, in Cornwall. This offers the rare sight of one of its Class 70 locomotives in the county. On 31 May 2017, No. 70815 approaches Liskeard with the inbound loaded working.

Initially, the loco ran round its train in Liskeard in order to reach the branch line to Moorswater and Looe. More recently it has continued west and carried out this run-round in Lostwithiel goods loop. No. 70815 is seen in this view, heading westbound through Liskeard station.

Following its run-round at Lostwithiel, No. 70815 approaches from the west and, after passing through the platform, is about to take the curve onto the Looe branch.

It then waits on the curve at Liskeard to follow the Looe branch diesel multiple unit. Once that unit is 'locked' into the section from Coombe Junction to Looe, the Class 70 can then continue its own journey to Moorswater. Its load on this occasion was eleven PCA wagons. It cleared the shared section of line before the unit was due to return from the Looe terminus.

Again in 2014, this time on 31 March, Freightliner Class 70s were regular performers on the short working between Bescot Yard and Washwood Heath concrete sleeper depot. The outbound trip was, on this occasion, a light engine. No. 70005 is seen passing through Walsall, heading for the Sutton Park line.

Back in 2013 it was a familiar sight to see Class 70s performing on almost-daily ballast workings between Crewe and Mountsorrel in Leicestershire. Not so today. On 16 April 2013, No. 70006 has left the Leicestershire quarry with its load and is seen heading through Burton-on-Trent. It will join the WCML at Lichfield.

Freightliner examples of Class 70s are becoming rarer in the Bristol area. On 16 July 2015, No. 70002 is a fortunate capture on an unidentified light engine move seen near Bath Spa station.

The Monday to Thursday infrastructure train linking Westbury, Hinksey and Bescot yards remains a popular 'one to see' for enthusiasts. This is due to it regularly producing at least one Class 70 in charge. Sometimes the wagon enthusiasts are not so handsomely rewarded as it often produces just a handful of wagons. This shot of No. 70802 on 17 March 2015 is a good example.

The capability of the same loco, No. 70802, was not exactly tested on 2 March 2017. Another short rake passes through Nuneaton station.

On 1 September 2014, it's a different date, a different loco, but still another short rake. No. 70805 is doing the honours, passing Nuneaton with a disappointing consist for the wagon enthusiasts.

On 2 June 2014, the working may have been of no interest whatsoever to the wagon enthusiasts. It did however raise a few eyebrows when No. 66847 appeared leading a three-loco convoy that included Class 70s numbered 70804 and 70802. They are seen waiting the signal at Nuneaton.

The Class 70 Freightliner fleet has been allowed to stretch its legs on the Anglo-Scottish workings between Daventry and Coatbridge. On 12 April 2016, No. 70011 passes through Tamworth's low level platforms heading towards Daventry on the southbound working.

The same working is seen through Tamworth's low level platforms three weeks later. No. 70003 heads south on 5 May 2016 with the liner from Coatbridge to Daventry.

The date is 21 February 2017 and this time it's a northbound working. No. 70015 heads for Coatbridge through Tamworth low level. At the time of this book's production, these services remain predominantly in the hands of Freightliner Class 90 Electric Locomotives.

The high level platforms at Tamworth also see the occasional Class 70 movement. On 20 October 2014, No. 70013 passes through on a service from Leeds to Southampton.

Several examples of Colas's fleet of seventeen locos can usually be seen in Hinksey Yard, particularly at weekends. This yard, on the southern outskirts of Oxford, was home to five class members on 1 May 2017, which was a Bank Holiday Monday. Nos 70810, 70811 and 70812 were stabled on one line as seen in this view.

In between the customary Network Rail foliage in full growth at this time of year, No. 70805 can be seen on the left with No. 70810 on the right.

The other member of the newly delivered batch, No. 70813, was stabled on a rake of autoballasters at the north (Oxford) end of the yard.

No. 70805 had been lined up to work that day's infrastructure working northward from Hinksey to Bescot. It was to have two cranes for company.

The Freightliner depot at Southampton Maritime was host to four members of the class over the Bank Holiday weekend of 29 and 30 April 2017. On the Sunday morning, No. 70019 was stabled complete with its rake of container flats adjacent to Redbridge station just beyond the depot.

On the depot itself, No. 70014 is in full view from the road bridge that same Sunday morning.

The other two examples present were partially hidden by the depot buildings. Here, No. 70011 is sandwiched between another class member, No. 70005, and Class 66 number 66548.

These two locos, No. 70005 and No. 70011, are also seen in this view from the access road bridge.

In addition to the two Freightliner examples that made an appearance on the afternoon of 5 May 2016 at Nuneaton, Colas was not to be outdone. The Westbury to Bescot infrastructure working produced another three Class 70s. These were hauled 'dead in train' behind No. 66850. The consist included, in order, No. 70805, No. 70806 and No. 70802.

This is the same working from a different angle. It was a Thursday and that day often produces multiple locos in connection with the following weekend's engineering work if any is taking place around the West Midlands.

There's always a buzz when a new, or nearly new, loco makes an appearance. Not long after its arrival on these shores, No. 70812 heads through Nuneaton on 27 March 2017, bound for Bescot, with a crane within the consist on its journey from Westbury via Hinksey.

Cranes are regularly conveyed in this particular working. On 26 January 2015, No. 70803 is in charge of the Bescot-bound working. On this occasion, Volker Rail crane No. DR81601 is supported by two runner wagons as it passes through Nuneaton.

With only nineteen Freightliner Class 70 locos out on the network, spotting them from a passing train is something of a challenge. Here, on 27 April 2017, No. 70008 is seen pausing alongside Brent Sidings at Willesden on its journey from Trafford Park to Felixstowe. It is again seen while passing on an adjacent line on a Milton Keynes to East Croydon service.

Freightliner has a substantial presence in the area around Crewe. Views of Basford Hall from a passing train are limited. Here, on 4 May 2017, No. 70007 is glimpsed from a Class 350 unit on the WCML. Also visible is Class 66 No. 66555.

Here's another view taken through the window of a Class 350 unit. This time it's No. 70018, on 18 October 2016, outside the Freightliner terminal at Ditton (Widnes).

On 3 September 2015, No. 70019 is seen alongside Doncaster's Up Decoy Yard waiting to head south on a liner. This time the view is taken from the window of a Class 153 diesel multiple unit working between Doncaster and Gainsborough.

Here is a snapshot of a week in the life of a Colas Class 70. In this case the loco is No. 70811 and these photos are taken between 15 April and 21 April 2017. On 15 April, No. 70811 is to be found in Hinksey yard in the company of a resident Class 08 shunter and Class 66s No. 66111 and No. 66560.

15 April 2017 was Easter Saturday. No. 70811 left Hinksey after this photo was taken and headed for Cardiff Canton. It was to remain there until 20 April.

On 20 April it headed north again and this time it was a light engine move from Cardiff Canton to Rugby. It is seen here approaching Nuneaton as it is about to head south on the WCML.

The following day, 21 April 2017, it was time for No. 70811 to head off again. Leaving Rugby light engine, it reversed at Nuneaton (where it was again photographed) before heading back to Hinksey Yard from where it had started its adventure seven days earlier.

Leeds, Yorkshire and the North East are served by several daily Freightliner services to and from both Felixstowe and Southampton. The terminal is located at Stourton in the Leeds suburbs. Felixstowe-bound services are routed via Doncaster and Peterborough. On 26 January 2016, No. 70016 heads north through Grantham with the Leeds-bound service from Felixstowe.

Less than two hours later and the same working passes round the back of Doncaster station.

On 17 June 2015, No. 70011 heads in the opposite direction. It is seen here crossing the East Coast Main Line running lines as it approaches Peterborough station. It will then head east to Felixstowe.

Southampton-bound services from Leeds's Stourton Terminal are routed via Chesterfield and through the West Midlands. On 13 October 2014, No. 70016 approaches Chesterfield on a southbound liner.

On 9 May 2017, another newly delivered loco, No. 70815, made its first appearance on the Westbury to Bescot infrastructure train. It is seen here as it passes through the centre road at Leamington Spa station. It will then take the Coventry line as it snakes through the West Midlands to reach Bescot Yard.

Coventry station is a busy bottleneck, which this working has to negotiate if it follows its usual routing. This involves crossing the busy WCML tracks in order to reach the Nuneaton branch. On 27 April 2015, No. 70807 comes off the curve into Coventry station. Again, two cranes are at the front of the consist.

Having then passed through Nuneaton, the service has to cross the Birmingham to Derby line at Water Orton to take the Sutton Park freight-only line. On 5 June 2014, No. 70809 is in charge as it passes Water Orton station.

By the time the train appears through the gloom at Walsall station it is approaching journey's end. On 29 April 2014, No. 70803 passes through on its final leg.

Colas locos of contrasting ages were seen in tandem through Tamworth's high level platforms on 28 June 2017. No. 70801 dragged No. 47739 from Washwood Heath to Barrow Hill (near Chesterfield). The veteran Class 47 was numbered D1615 when first built and is nearly half a century older than the Class 70.

On 29 June 2017, No. 70812 was seen passing Doncaster station on the two-way goods line. It was working light engine from Bescot to Barnetby, South Humberside. Class 70s had briefly appeared on tank trains from Humberside during 2016, as evidenced later in this book. Would this loco move see them return to such duties?

Light engine moves are often necessary between Freightliner's various terminals in the UK. One such instance occurred on 1 February 2016 (a Monday) when No. 70020 was seen heading south onto the WCML. The loco had left Lawley Street (Birmingham), where it had presumably spent the weekend, and was running to Daventry to collect its train.

Light engine moves between the various yards within the town of Crewe often see reversals in the bay platforms normally reserved for the local Shrewsbury services. In the bay platform on 30 October 2014, No. 70017 is seen on one such loco reversal. On this occasion, the mixed assortment of locos also consisted of No. 90046, No. 86613 and No. 86638.

The loco holding sidings just south of Doncaster station are often home to one or two Colas locos. These can be from any of the classes that form their motive power fleet. On 23 March 2015, No. 70806 was stabled there in the company of one of Colas Rail's small pool of five Class 66 locos, No. 66850. The previous day these two locos had top-and-tailed a ballast train from Barrow Hill into Doncaster's Decoy Yard. The Class 70 was back at Hoo Junction two days later.

Two years later, on 5 May 2017, newly delivered No. 70816 was to be found in the same location. It had been part of a light engine move that saw it leave Seaforth Docks and head to Bescot Yard. It continued alone, reaching here the previous evening. It was en route to be based at Barnetby prior to a revenue-earning run two weeks later on the tanks from Lindsey Oil Refinery to Rectory Junction (Nottingham).

Colas Class 70 locomotives were used briefly on the aviation fuel tank workings between Lindsey, on South Humberside, and Colnbrook (near Heathrow). This was routed via the southern section of the Midland Main Line. On 17 June 2016, No. 70808 was in charge. It is seen here accelerating north from Bedford station on the return working of the empties. It had just crew-changed in the station. As this publication closed, a Class 70 (No. 70802) was outbased at Grangemouth for hauling similar tank workings in Scotland.

Two years earlier, the same loco, No. 70808, was in more familiar surroundings. On 25 November 2014, it has just been given the road to take the curve westward from Nuneaton station as it heads to Bescot with the Infrastructure working from Westbury.

The Trent Valley section of the WCML remains one of the best areas for Freightliner Class 70 sightings. On 16 March 2016, No. 70009 heads through Rugby with a Felixstowe to Lawley Street (Birmingham) working. This train will veer west off the Trent Valley at Nuneaton to reach its terminal.

Further north, on 13 April 2016, No. 70014 passes through Tamworth's low level platforms with a southbound working. This time it's a Crewe to Felixstowe service, which was routed via the WCML to the London suburbs in order to reach the Suffolk port.

By contrast, this northbound working from Felixstowe has taken advantage of the new curve at Europa Junction in Ipswich. It has then travelled cross-country through East Anglia, reaching the WCML at Nuneaton via Peterborough and Leicester. This Crewe-bound liner is in the hands of No. 70008 on 9 February 2017. It is seen approaching Nuneaton, coming off the Leicester line.

A heavy downpour greets No. 70017 at it reaches Stafford on 8 June 2016. On this occasion, it has travelled via the West Midlands to join the WCML here on a Southampton to Garston (Merseyside) service.

Stafford was again the location for this working on 28 June 2017. No. 70007 headed a container train southbound through the station on its way from Trafford Park to Southampton.

Water Orton, on the outskirts of Birmingham, sees Class 70 appearances from both operators. On 22 July 2014, the station witnessed the passing of a pair of Colas locos. No. 70808 led sister No. 70810 as they headed west through the station. They would shortly take the freight-only line via Sutton Park to reach Bescot Yard with their rake of JNAs from Westbury.

There can be few occasions when Class 70 locomotives have been hired in by the 'opposition'. That certainly seemed to be the case on 23 April 2014. Colas-operated No. 70809 was called upon to handle a Freightliner working from Aldwarke to Crewe; it is seen here heading south through Chesterfield with a rake of open scrap wagons (SSAs).

A Freightliner example of the class is seen here on an aggregate working on 10 November 2014. No. 70010 passes through the centre of Doncaster station with a return working from Eggborough power station to Tunstead. Its load is a rake of empty aggregate hoppers (HIAs).

Since that photo was taken, Doncaster has seen a downturn in freight traffic routed through its station area. On 29 June 2017, No. 70019 made a welcome appearance on that morning's Felixstowe to Leeds freightliner container train. It is seen using the two-way goods line adjacent to the station's platforms.

It was a damp morning in the West Midlands on 22 October 2013. No. 70009 passes east through Coleshill Parkway with a service from Lawley Street to Felixstowe.

Brush Traction often undertakes work on Freightliner's loco fleet at its works at Loughborough. On 24 October 2013, No. 70007 had been dispatched to Loughborough to collect No. 66518 following attention there. It is seen dragging the Class 66 through Nuneaton as the two engines are returning light engine to their base at Basford Hall in Crewe.

Freightliner often uses its service trains as a means of moving locos between its various operating and servicing bases. It is a common sight to see a mixture of different class types in this mode. For example, on the afternoon of 16 May 2017, No. 90046 is in charge of a Trafford Park to Felixstowe working. It is conveying No. 70017 'dead in train' as it passes south through Nuneaton.

At least at the time of this compilation, Colas Rail's regular weekday duties are limited in the main to their handful of infrastructure workings to and from the yards at Hoo Junction and Westbury. None attracts more interest than the Westbury to Bescot service documented in this book. For the wagon enthusiasts, it offers a variety of engineering wagons, as these views again demonstrate. On 12 June 2017, No. 70811 has a rake of JNAs heading towards Bescot.

On 4 January 2016, No. 70805 makes an appearance at Nuneaton along with a rake of bogie ballast and aggregate hoppers.

On 16 January 2017, No. 70806 heads through the Nuneaton platform. Much to the relief of the enthusiasts hoping to log the numbers of the 'salmon' in the consist, it crawled up to a red signal before heading west.

No joy, however, for such enthusiasts on 16 May 2017. No. 70809 put in a nil return on the wagon front as it headed west light engine to Bescot.

In mid-2017, the Freightliner Class 70 locomotives are mainly confined to container traffic out of both Felixstowe and Southampton. This means, of course, that they make frequent appearances on the southern section of the WCML. On 9 May that year, No. 70003 works a Felixstowe-bound liner through Nuneaton. This working was from Ditton on Merseyside.

On 21 April 2017, No. 70006 approaches Bletchley station on another Felixstowe-bound service. This southbound working had left Trafford Park in Manchester earlier that morning.

Services from the terminals in the North West of England are often subject to loco changes at Basford Hall yard in Crewe. This Trafford Park to Felixstowe working on 21 March 2016 was one such example. It is seen southbound through Stafford. The loco, No. 70008, had taken the service forward from Crewe.

On 2 March 2017, No. 70019 is routed via Nuneaton on a service from Southampton to Garston (Merseyside). This working has also been regularly routed via the West Midlands rather than the Trent Valley. On this occasion it is slowing at Nuneaton for a crew change before continuing north.

Several daily Freightliner services operate to and from the International Rail Freight Terminal at Daventry in Northamptonshire. These include services to and from Southampton. Some of these liners use the WCML to Wembley and then reach Reading via Acton, while others leave Reading West and reach Daventry via Oxford and Birmingham. On 15 April 2017, No. 70015 is seen passing alongside Hinksey yard, south of Oxford, with a Daventry-bound working.

On 23 June 2016, No. 70010 is using the WCML to reach Reading and onwards to Southampton. It is seen approaching Bletchley station.

In March 2017, Class 70s took their turn on the Anglo-Scottish workings between the rail-linked sites at Daventry and Coatbridge. These services are operated on behalf of Russell Logistics. On 2 March 2017, the Coatbridge-bound service heads north through Nuneaton behind No. 70015.

On 21 March 2017, it's the turn of No. 70008 to handle this Daventry to Coatbridge working. On this occasion, the train is given the use of the 'Down fast' as it passes through Nuneaton station.

At weekends, Colas Rail's Class 70s can be seen almost anywhere on the network depending on where infrastructure work is taking place. On 21 September 2014, No. 70808 had been dispatched from Whitemoor Yard (near March in Cambridgeshire) to an engineering possession at Sleaford in Lincolnshire. It is seen at Marholm, just north of Peterborough, on the ECML.

On 15 April 2015, Colas Rail had a number of its Class 70s employed on infrastructure duties in the area west of Paddington station. These trains were worked to and from Hinksey yard, south of Oxford. They included No. 70813 on one of its first outings since arriving in the UK. It is seen returning from Ladbroke Grove to Hinksey that afternoon when captured at South Moreton, to the east of Didcot Parkway.

It is a regular occurrence for the Colas Class 70 working their Westbury to Bescot infrastructure train to reach Nuneaton at the same time as the DB Cargo-operated Halewood to Southampton car train. On 20 February 2017, it is the turn of No. 70810 to meet No. 66113, operating the Southampton-bound car train.

In June 2017, the four new Colas machines continued to attract much attention among enthusiasts. News broke early on 20 June when No. 70817 was reported leaving Westbury on the Colas Infrastructure working to Bescot. By mid-afternoon, when the loco passed through Nuneaton, there was a bigger than usual gathering to witness its second appearance (I believe) on this working. A Kirow crane was again at the head of the consist.

As 2017 began, several Freightliner Class 70s remained out of use at Leeds Midland Road depot. These locos are seen in these four shots taken on 25 January that year. The depot is adjacent to the Leeds to Woodlesford line and on this date the locos were lined up alongside the depot fence. Approaching from the south, No. 70009 leads the line-up.

On the morning of 25 January 2017, the depot was home to half of its fleet, including the stored line-up. No. 70006 is seen next to the fence here within the line-up. This particular loco was not included in the 'official' stored list of Nos 70001, 70002, 70003, 70009, 70013 and 70014.

This shot shows No. 70002 very much constrained in this line-up, which was again viewed from a passing Class 158 on the Woodlesford line.

The same goes for No. 70003, featured here next to No. 70002. Despite being hemmed in, the future was much brighter for this loco a few months later.

Fast forward to 18 May 2017 and there have been some changes to the locos lined up alongside the depot fence that morning. This shot was taken from the Pepper Road bridge to the south of the depot. The locos are Nos 70009 (nearest camera), 66533, 70013, 70018, 70016, 70001, 70002 and 90041 (at the north end).

As mentioned above, No. 70001 now finds itself hemmed in within this line, as seen here once again from a passing service on the Woodlesford line.

Aside from the line-up of six stored locos, Midland Road was home to four more members of the class on the morning of 18 May 2017. One of these was No. 70010, seen here at the buffer stops at the Balm Road (north) end of the depot.

Across the car park near the depot entrance was No. 70011. This loco was about to move off to the nearby Freightliner terminal to take charge of a southbound liner.

In 2017, Colas Rail commenced a new freight flow from Abbey Wharf, Neath (South Wales). Serving destinations at Washwood Heath (Birmingham) and Leeds Stourton, these workings are normally hauled by Class 70s, although a pair of Class 56s did handle the inaugural run to Leeds at the end of April. On 8 June 2017, No. 70814 provided the power. It is seen at Chesterfield on the southbound working from Leeds.

The company has received a rake of former coal hoppers (HHAs) to handle this flow. The wagons had been in long-term storage for Freightliner at Donnington. On reaching South Wales, they will stable in Briton Ferry Yard until their next call of duty at Neath.

The same working is seen later in its southbound journey later that day. The rake of empties is captured as it approaches Burton-on-Trent behind No. 70814.

Here is another view of No. 70814 as it nears Burton-on-Trent station. The station sign proudly promotes Burton as: 'A gateway to the National Forest'. It begins at both of the platform ends!